To James
with love
from

To James,
with love,
♡ Mam x
1/12/24

Mary Emeji

MULTIVERSE

Where dreams become reality....

GlintingBlue Press

ISBN: 978-0-9928162-7-8
MMXXIV

Printed and bound in Great Britain.
First published in Great Britain in 2024
By
GlintingBlue Press
glintingbluepress1@yahoo.co.uk

CONTENTS

46. MULTIVERSE ADVENTURE

47. Multiverse-On-Sea
48. Sky High
49. Palacio Real De la Almudaina
50. Castell De Bellver
51. Playa De Portals
53. Angel Sweets
54. Home To Hove
55. Galaxy Walk
56. Praia Do Vau
57. Midnight In Paris
58. Composed Upon Sunset In Paris
60. Moon Inside
61. Lake Geneva
62. Wonderful Corfu
63. Costa Del Sol

64. MULTIVERSE OF LOVE

65. Quantum Of Love
66. Tree Of Beauty
67. Multiverse Of Love
68. The Love Magnet
70. The Other Us
71. Nature Talks
72. The Comet
74. Dream With Me
75. The Wonder Of Waiting
76. Forever Love
77. The Time Apart
79. Love's Inferno
80. Angel Dance
81. Like It Never Ends
82. Summer Walk

83. MULTIVERSE INFINITY

84. Light In The Sun
85. Mary's Multiverse
86. High Flyer
88. Dream Into Timelines
89. The Multiverse Cake
90. Letter To Me
91. Self-Love
92. Multiverse Of Me Time
93. Angel In The Wind
94. Usurped By Light
95. Walkway Runway
97. Serendipity
98. Christmas Stars
99. Music From The Multiverse
100. Stairway To Light
101. Ferry Me Across The Multiverse

ABOUT THE AUTHOR

Mary Emeji is the Poet Laureate of Luton and Founder of the very first Luton Poetry Society since 2011, and she coordinates monthly poetry events at Luton Central Library. A double law graduate with LLB(Hons) and LLM Commercial Law (with Distinction) from University of Bedfordshire, Mary's passion for poetry leads her to perform in libraries, festivals and events around the UK and abroad. The 'six books in six years' poet regularly appears on BBC Three Counties Radio, as well as in Bedfordshire local newspapers and magazines including Herald & Post, Luton News, Luton On Sunday, and Luton-at-Large. Mary was the guest speaker on ITV News for International Women's Day 2021. Mary has won poetry competitions, including 'National Poetry Anthology Competition 2012' and 'Top Ten Poets in the UK 2013' organised by United Press. Mary received an award from Luton Mayor Cllr. Tahir Khan for "Outstanding contribution to poetry in Luton" in 2017, and in 2018 she received the High Sheriff of Bedfordshire's Citizenship Award for her "Great and Valuable Services to the Luton Community." Mary was the guest poet representing Great Britain in the Switzerland festival *Seetaler Poesiesommer* in August 2018. Mary won the Luton's Best Adult Achiever award in 2020 and her photo appears in Luton's landmark photomosaic located in Silver Street, Luton, Bedfordshire.

"Mary is the life and soul of Luton Poetry Society. She charms and enchants us with her appearance, personality and theatrical performances of poems, sometimes accompanied by lovely well-chosen classical music."
--Francis McDonnell

OTHER BOOKS BY MARY:
THE BOND OF LOVE (2009), THE LOVE OF GOD (2010), ROYAL LUMINOSITY (2011 - *Dedicated to Prince William and Kate, and received a royal acknowledgement from HM The Queen)*, TIMELESS DATE (2012 *Co-written with William Shakespeare)*, FUNDAMENTALITY (2013), PULCHRITUDE (2014), MY FRIEND THE SUN (2016) and THE ISLAND (2019).

REVIEWS

Mary's poetry has an enchanting flow and an arresting rhythm. When a reader gets into the zone of this writing, he or she will feel these qualities as strongly as when Mary performs her work, which she does wonderfully. I find this poet's work charming, humorous and thoughtful, as well as embracing themes of genuine spirituality and love that will certainly resonate with believers.
~~Neil Rowland – Poet, Novelist and Writer

The voice of Mary Emeji is one of the authentic poet. This authenticity of who and what we are and the beautiful spaces in between of just simply being, envelops the reader like a gentle stream and also like a cascading waterfall. Mary's performance poetry always imparts something of her beautiful and spiritual self.
~~Hilda Morley – Poet

Mary is such an honest poet who simply follows her heart – and to hear her verses is to know that her love of life is perfectly served by her love of language.
~~Richard Sisson – Poet, Pianist, Composer, Manager at Luton Music Club

"Mary is an inspirational poet, her poetry conveys good traditional values and her words flow from the heart. I feel privileged to have met the Poet Laureate of Luton. Mary's faith and commitment to poetry will give pleasure to many readers in the future."
--Lady Isabelle, The Countess of Erroll

PREFACE

The beauty of any mystery shines in the impossibility of fully understanding it. So does the beauty of the Multiverse. The infinite possibilities are to be experienced, not understood. In this book, the Multiverse is experienced with joy and love! Multiverse celebrates Mary's 15th anniversary of being an author, a journey of self-discovery leading to infinity. The poems are complemented with picturesque art by Mary.

History records apparitions of angels to Mary, Joseph, Tobias and the Magi who followed a star to find baby Jesus. Various saints had the gift of bilocation (ability to be in two places simultaneously) and multilocation (ability to be in multiple places simultaneously) including St. Pio, St. Alphonsus Liguori, and others. The ancient King Solomon and St. Francis could communicate with animals and the rest of nature.

God spoke to many in dreams. Joseph had the ability to dream and his dreams always became reality. Could they have already been reality at the point of dreaming? We know that at the point of dreaming, everything feels as reality. Perhaps dreams are a window into the Multiverse?

The reader is invited to dream big and be limitless. Multiverse is where dreams become reality. We can time travel to various versions of us, for instance to the inner child to remember how amazing we are. The poems reflect on the alter ego within and in the Multiverse. To find one's inner self leads to wholeness and happiness.

In Quantum physics, our thought patterns create our reality. For every dream we really believe, the universe connects with the mind to bring it to reality. The quantum theory asserts that all possible outcomes are not just possibilities but are actualities in other realms.

Think of the multiplicity of your shadows under the sun, your reflection in the waters of the sea, the rainfall and snowfall from the sky, the singing birds and the musical wind. In the beauty of nature all around us, imagination meets creation.

In religion, God is omnipresent everywhere, every time, and since we are God's children created in God's image and likeness, we inherit a bit of the transcendental gift from God. Jesus said, if we have faith the size of a mustard seed, we can move mountains. Nothing is impossible. *(Matthew 17:20-21).*

We can expand our daily thinking to the infinite realm and harness the inner power that God gives us and thereon to be the best of us every time, everywhere for all time.

FOREWORD

To see a world in a grain of sand
And heaven in a wildflower
Hold infinity in the palm of your hand
And eternity in an hour.
(William Blake, Auguries of Inncocence, 1.1)

Through the Multiverse Mary shares her life's journey, her thoughts, dreams and reality.

As Einstein followed the sunbeam, to discover his theory of relativity, so mass at a certain speed of light turns into energy. The light refracts into photons and the world appears a duality of light and darkness, hot and cold.

Stephen Hawking developed his ideas of the universe with black holes, massive stars collapsing, which it was speculated, could lead to other universes. Hence the multiverse was proposed.

Hugh Everett III developed these ideas from the quantum physics analysis of photons through space and time as every quantum passes separate universes for each outcome.

Mary takes us through her dreams to life's difficult moments with a strong faith in the guiding hand of the Spirit, to discover the inner self. First the appreciation of finding the diversity within the 'little world inside you', the trials and through the wonder of the elements, the sky, sun and space where you find transcendence. She finds 'her talents grow and glow like a divine prayer'.

Her travels take her to Lake Geneva, Paris, Corfu and the Palacio Real de la Almudaina in Majorca, Spain where 'poetry muse led' her where she finds herself 'a Queen in her own multiverse to reign'. So from dreams to reality. Boldness is required to find the 'true essence of effulgence'.

In the 'quantum of love' is found the complementarity in which 'true love is perfected'. The light of the sun leads her to the light of the imagination across the multiverse infinity through faith into actuality where she finds 'God within'.

Alan Rainer, Poet, Philosopher
(October 2024)

DEDICATION

♥ For my Angel of all time ♥

EFFULGENCE

The true essence
Of effulgence
Is not demureness
But boldness.

ALTER-EXISTENCE

Another place
Another time,
Another face
Another life:

One not seen
One not sad,
Come with me
To wonderland.

BIRD AND BREAKFAST

I hear the birds from my window singing
As my first sunrise coffee I'm drinking.
Morning classical music on the radio is playing
My friend the sun her light is shinning.

The tall leafy trees to me are waving
In the gentle wind of springtime morning.
Coffee in hand and a homemade cookie eating,
I feel the elements of nature connecting.

I take time to enjoy this moment elevating,
Rising with the sun to the realms of dreaming.
I treasure the beauty of nature enchanting
My quintessence to be strong and keep going.

I live on the Island of serenity overflowing
From within to the picturesque view inspiring.
Bird and breakfast is my delightful routine
That sets me to take on the day ever smiling.

INNER-OUTER

I'm sitting on the pavement,
Peering into the boulevard
Of timelessness and puzzlement
Drifting the mind afar;

And all is frozen, suddenly still,
But deep inside, I'm rising, scampering
From pouring sun to cascading chill
And everywhere my heart is choosing.

I can visit, re-visit or plan to visit
The moments of joy and hopeful dreams,
Preceding roads and seasons in transit;
I can seamlessly swim in emotion's stream.

Everything opens and closes within:
The path to all I desire to find.
From limited bodies, we play the violin
Of secret travel in pulchritudinous mind.

CROSSROADS

The crossroads running through existence
Intercept at various points of luminescence.
Turn on the lights under the bright sunlight
They deem since the sun is supreme light.

We need to connect to the realm of multiverse
To see our versatility and be diverse.
There is more to me than meets the eye
All of me united will triumph beyond the sky.

The star lights illuminate the sky at midnight
You sleep and simultaneously awaken to light.
The light in the multiverse crosses through portals
Like the unveiling of curtains at the movie halls.

The light is in you and every time you step out
Of the comfort zone and shed off the doubt,
You open up endless possibilities of brightness.
Lights intertwined in crossroads of the multiverse.

TRAGIC TO MAGIC

Doom, derision, distress, depression
Life makes you question its own confusion.
Sickness, seclusion, selfish segregation
But in that time, you can make a decision.

Stand up for yourself, be true to your existence!
Life is not confusion at its very essence.
Oh no! The seasons come in their sequence
And one by one they become past tense.

But you are the present, peaceful, pulchritude
You are endowed with beauty and fortitude.
From tragic to magic, you find your plenitude
Rise higher and shine in multiversal magnitude.

Oh that smile looks so good on you today
Do what you can to be happy every day.
Life is beautiful and magic is your way.
Let go of the tragic and live your life I say!

ANGEL DUST

From inner streams within my soul
I saw her light reflecting:
Felt her touch of love alone
And life in me attesting.

It wasn't quite noon for summer rays
To capture such great light,
Or the moon at night to seek some praise
In her gleaming frock of white.

She mellowed into my heartbeat
And danced with me awhile
And sprinkled shimmering dust in fleet,
Before she walked the mile.

I searched through snow and daffodils
But my eyes could not reclaim
The sight of her on lonely hills,
Until she called my name.

I look on her with love and trust
And not a tearful eye,
For wherever she sprinkled the angel dust
The light will shine for aye!

RAIN SHOWER

God's Spirit can take away
Your pain and all your fears allay.
His blessings like the rain shower
Renews you with divine power.

The outpour of His graces divine
Washes my mind to celestial shine.
Fount of love and mercy immeasurable
Rains on me with blessings innumerable.

Asperges me, Domine, my Lord
Let pain be gone and health restored.
That all of me will rejuvenate
To newness with joy to scintillate.

So I levitate to the quantum sky
Of endless love and grace to vivify.
God's Spirit from the very onset
Gives life to all, sunrise to sunset.

(Words in Italics translate to "Wash me, Lord")

START - STOP - START AGAIN

Oh! you didn't think I will make it this time
Well, its start - stop - and start again.
Through all that doubt and pain decline
I hit the stop button twice to start again.

Yes, the same button you press to stop
Is the same button you push to start.
To decide to stop and again stop
Is to stop stopping and again start!

So chase that dream you always had
The dream you deferred for compromise.
Start today, right now and you will be glad
To find reward in your skilful enterprise!

The way appears the moment you step forth
Not always before, so your best time is now.
Brace up and take the great leap of faith
Trusting yourself and not questioning how!

THE LIFE I SEE

As I sit and meditate
Upon the mid-day stream,
I gaze on the bright sun of mortality
That outshines the reality of dreams.
I realise, that life is more than I see.

The strips of the veil of physicality
Part open before the eyes of my soul;
As I feel the gentle breeze of my life,
The condiments of existence that make me whole,
Waving through the past, present and future.

I try to catch the rain of memories
In the cup I hold in my palm today,
That I may water the deserted lands
And plant green leaves on tomorrow's way.
I play the piano of destiny, to my desired tune.

But life is deeper than the wishes of the mind.
Uncontrolled by the times and seasons that go by.
Life to me is how I choose to perceive
The daily puzzles of wonder and why.
My serenity remains deep in my heart!

PERSONAL FOCUS

Connect with your inner child today
Remember the innocence and joyful play;
How you had no worry or dark dismay
And everything good will come your way.

So when and why did you give it away
Your trust and love on dark winter's day?
Take it back, take it all back I say.
You deserve much better than disarray.

Would you neglect your child anyway
Or would you love and nurture her everyday?
So take the love inside you like dazzling ray
And shine it all on yourself each day.

Then you will be equipped on summer's day
To spread magnificence as you walk the way.
Protect your inner child from doom and grey.
Shine light and dazzle on dreamers' way.

IN SEARCH OF THE MULTIVERSE

I long for you in this universe
The other me and all the others.
I know that in the worlds out there
You're real - the dreams I hold so dear.

The challenge today is draining
I feel stuck in the clouds and it's raining.
The portal of the multiverse opens up
For a second to see the possibilities.

I am not curtailed by pain and sorrow
The life I desire will come tomorrow.
I will do my best in the present state
To keep us happy and to rejuvenate.

So I connect with you today my love
The other me, with you I am enough.
All of us together in a timeless embrace
Emit positive energy to light up the face.

I am happy and strong as I can be
My life is fixed and I am healed.
The heroic sacrifice has gained reward.
I am whole, empowered and restored.

ALL THINGS BRIGHT

Just before my classical music began to play
I heard the voice of the wind sing woohoo.
I'm having first coffee on this beautiful Sunday
The sunshine scintillates everything anew.

In the multiverse the glow is moonshine
Shimmering softly across the endless sky
All of me is aglow with the moon or sunshine.
I am light, I am transcending way up high.

Light up the fire of passion for success:
Dream-chaser dream-catcher is my motto.
The moon in the sun is greater happiness
Candlelight shines resilient in her grotto.

The light in the light is connecting my light
The moonshine of magical stars floating by.
The gusty wind with her singing so bright
Dazzles me this Sunday morning to glorify.

MOON

I'm watching the moon in the sky moving
Or is it just the clouds shifting?
There's moon in my eyes, softly reflected
In beams by which we are connected.

What sees you is what you see:
Eye to eye, drawing from within.
No word or sound could ever suffice
The visual sentiment starting to rise.

You're a planet, somewhere beyond
But from my window, I see a bond
That requires no shuttle or astronaut
To conclude the love that we have caught.

Surrounded by clouds, with light blue spine
Encircling the circumference of your shine,
I fall asleep with moon on my mind
And you in my eyeballs redesigned.

ANGEL OF LIGHT

God of the night you make my heart bright
You give me peace and incredible might.
Through the stormy sea, I let go of fright
I trust you to send me the Angel of light.

God of the morning, you show me sunlight
As I'm drinking my first coffee with delight.
You renew me with reflection on celestial height.
With the Angel of light, my day will be alright.

God of the noon, you're my King and Knight
You shield me from woe, yours is the fight.
The grey clouds give way to reveal skylight.
She holds me close my Angel of light.

God of the evening, thank you for inner sight
My poetry and bakery talents you always ignite.
A decade of love poems to my Angel of light:
You lead me day and night into the eternal light.

TIME TRAVEL

The moment of realisation that memory
Is a time machine recreating history,
Leads one to sit back and reflect anew
On the paths that led to the present view.

For time is memory and memory time
We can harness the joy of life sublime.
Close your eyes and dream into that place
That you have been in time and space.

The holidays wonder, the success celebration,
Everywhere every time that you found elation.
Photographic memory brings you merriment
From past to present and future wonderment.

We have the gift of mindfulness meditation
To experience realities beyond imagination.
So time travel into the multiverse of possibilities.
Where you find your dreams become reality.

TRANSCENDENCE

There's a little world inside you
Unseen to the eyes, felt deep inside
Like a gust of wind breezing through.
From nowhere, the elements start to collide:

Protons, electrons, memories and forecasts
Swaying around in breeze propellant.
You're here and there, gravity surpassed
Like Lucy's brain capacity at 100 percent!

The wind is gusting but earth is still,
The visible world now becoming iridescent.
Your brain is soaring above trees and hills
To the sky high point where you're transcendent.

There, King Solomon's wisdom shines in corona.
Through the sun, the mind is fully energised.
Now you see and feel everything, the aura
So different from what the human eye disguised.

Behold the hidden secrets of the wind:
By air, we remit immeasurable quotient.
Yet when you start to doubt or rescind,
The inner world stops - and you forget!

(Lucy is a movie about the brain capacity reaching 100%)

CAUTION, CONTENTS HOT!

Caution, contents hot! That simply
Depicts me on this morning glee.
Having coffee in a cafe, I'm inspired
By this text on my coffee cup inscribed.

The view is picturesque by the window
Watching the morning sun set all aglow:
The spring flowers and enlivening green trees
And the gentle gust of the morning breeze.

I am hot in beauty and youthful essence,
Timeless and ageless in my rejuvenescence.
I follow my dreams with focus and passion
Poetry perfection and bakery celebration.

Somewhere in the multiverse it's lunchtime
And I'm having tapas with a glass of wine,
Out in the Spanish sun by the sea in Majorca.
Well, Luton airport is nearby, so see you later!

MULTIVERSE OF M

In my dreams I go on adventures,
Travel through time and space to discover
The multiverse of M in royal grandeur
My joy scintillates on greener pastures.

There is M the poet who writes from heart
And MM the baker who bakes you happy
Both multi-award winners in their originality.
Poetry is my light and bakery my art.

There's M the Mum devoted to offspring
And M the Queen, a woman of her own.
Yes, M the Adult Achiever of milestone
Connects all the M's to joyfully sing.

So I charm and enchant with happiness
I am my best self, I am magnificence.
My light shines around in eloquence
I am the multiverse of Mary-ness.

BIRTHDAY AT MIDNIGHT

Midnight now, happy birthday to me I say.
Thank you Lord for this bright new day
Heal me in every way, I pray.
Bless me Lord in a bright new way
On this merry Monday 20th of May.

BIRTHDAY QUEEN MARY

I am ageless and timeless
I am happiness and wholeness.
I embrace my uniqueness
I achieve resplendent success.

I am my greatest achievement
Being my true self without relent.
I walk my path less travelled by
To soar in authenticity above sky high.

Yes, it's my birthday to celebrate
With love and joy to scintillate.
I open the portal to rejuvenate
And all my dreams to activate.

I wear my crown with *Pulchritude*
Finesse, boldness and fortitude.
My *Multiverse* shines in *Royal Luminosity*
With *My Friend The Sun* in *Fundamentality*.

Yes, *The Bond Of Love* connecting all of me
Enkindles on a *Timeless Date* perfectly.
The Love Of God gives me serenity
On *The Island* to be the best of me.

(All my book titles in Italics. Happy 15th anniversary of authorship to me!)

ANGEL CAKE

I created a picturesque Angel cake
To enjoy in springtime beside the lake.
One taste of you and I am in heaven
Forgetting the trials that came in eleven.

Decorated with flowers pink and white
And white chocolate stars for Angel's light,
This chocolate cake brings much felicity.
My soul and spirit elevate in divinity.

I lost, then I found you deep in my heart.
You guide and guard, we're never apart.
We launched The Island one week ago
And now you're showing me the way to go.

Another taste of you, I'm on a date with you
On The Island with bright sun and sky blue.
Let's have some tea, dazzling Angel of mine.
Your sweet light in me will forever shine.

SIDES OF THE COIN

The parallel universe exists on the other side,
The clocks go forth and back at different times.
We hold hands and let go, we mirror the tide
Of the ocean of love and friendship sublime.

The crux of our quintessence is full of true love
With sparkles and sprinkles of smile and laughter.
Deep in your eyes I find treasure from above
And every moment we share makes us stronger.

We take a loving walk through the streets of snow
Admiring the bare trees and rooftops all white,
Walking into the summer gardens of sunshine aglow
At noonday on the other side of multiversal light.

Two sides of the same coin in the parallel existence,
Two sides of how you feel in the varying atmosphere.
Choose to stay true to your authentic quintessence
And find the versions of you all alight everywhere.

MULTIVERSAL SHINE

I drink the stars not with the stars
I shimmer and shine in my own light.
I don't need to adapt or search so far
When the star in me is shining bright.

The other me gently takes my hand
As we walk the path of great success.
I hear her and I begin to understand
That when I walk, the way appears.

A myriad of galaxies all connected
Meet my eyes in luminous grandeur
I dance with the starlight deeply reflected
In my dreams of a multiversal affair.

So I shine my light everywhere, every time
I am who I am and I cannot compare.
Unique, enchanted I live in my multiversal shine.
My talents grow and glow like a divine prayer.

ANGEL'S WINGS

I'm ready to fly high to reach my dreams
Atop the mountains and gentle streams.
My friend the sun is smiling bright
Inspiring my mind with novel light.

I found the way to my secret escape
Where I rise above the dim landscape.
I encounter the portal to the multiverse
Shining in the lines of my poetry verse.

I am empowered with my Angels wings
She wraps me with light and joyful rings.
I'm ready to achieve my deepest desire
Connecting with all of me in all I aspire.

The Angel in me has begun this journey
Of self-love and self-trust living victoriously.
I'm set to charm and enchant with happiness
By being my true self, I am magnificence.

LEAP YEAR DAY 2024

I have found the multiverse
The portal is open in my poetry verse.
On the leap year day, I now enjoy
The quantum of me in multiples of joy.

The grace and peace that God bestows
On me to venture where His spirit flows,
Reminds me that everywhere, every time
He's with me always to the end of time.

So here I am on leap year day 2024
The exceptional day - once in years of four,
When one reflects and makes great plans
To achieve marvellously by the next leap year.

I took an adventure of a great day out
A pleasant walk and a toast at The George.
I encounter the beauty of love and peace
And I pray that in God they never cease.

MULTIVERSITY

For every time you feel futility
Remember that you are infinity
Created in God's image and deity.
You inherit His divine immortality.

So search for inward clarity
Deep within your fundamentality.
You will unlock the infinite possibility
Of your talents exceeding multiplicity.

You can live in eternal multiversity
Right here in this vale of vanity,
Because you have the perspicacity
Of God's wisdom in your spirituality.

So break the walls of impossibility
To reach your boundless invincibility.
Harness your inner royal luminosity
Then sparkle and spark in perpetuity.

SUNRISE COFFEE

The sun is shining through the trees
Enlivening the landscape luminosity.
The birds are singing their morning song
Sweet tunes of beauty for which I long.

I am relaxing with the morning classical
Playing on my radio, it's peacefully magical.
Franz Liszt's "Un Suspiro" is playing now
My favourite piece of wonder and wow!

Buenos dias Mary, aqui esta tu café
My sunrise coffee for a happy new day!
I enjoy serenity every morning with glee:
Great view, singing birds, music and coffee.

I like my coffee hot, strong and flavoursome
No sugar, little milk and a dash of awesome.
I am whole and complete, I am eloquence.
I am multiversal, I am magnificence.

(Italics translate to "Morning Mary, here's your coffee.")

SUNSET TEA

The evening goes quiet when birds unwind,
When my friend the sun is settling behind
The picturesque landscape of a dreamy view.
At the end of the day, one can rest and renew.

Concierto de Aranjuez is playing on my radio
I feel the gentle wind seep through my window.
The music of my soul nourishes me with glee
As I enjoy my very nice cup of English tea.

A slice of my freshly baked madeira cake
Compliments my sunset tea, such joy to bake!
Everything comes together in this moment
When I have my relaxing tea at sunset.

Love yourself inside out without reserve
You just might a whole lifespan preserve.
Que sera sera, soy la reina abundancia
Soy luz, soy fuerte y soy magnificencia.

(Last two lines translate: "What will be will be, I am the abundant queen.
I am light, I am strong and I am magnificence.")

MOONSHINE WINE

For a little few minutes you were mine
The rare celestial pink moon sublime.
You appeared so huge in the sky tonight
Gleaming pink and orange rays of light.

Gently you rose from behind the clouds aglow
Just when I was looking out of the window.
I popped outside to catch a clear view fast
There was even an airplane flying past.

I walked with you in the moonshine
Relishing the magical moment in time,
Harnessing your energy in this universe
And transmitting out into the multiverse.

With all that glimmer and shimmer sublime
The other me is relaxing with moonshine wine.
My crystals are charging in celestial grandeur
My friend the moon, *bienvenida mi amor.*

Never doubt yourself - you are sublime!
I am clothed with light and beauty divine.
I am whole and complete I'm happy and bright.
My dreams come true under the moonlight.

(Italics translate: "Welcome, my love.")

MULTIVERSE-ON-SEA

Like the bird flying over the sea
I'm free to be everything I wish to be.
No place or time could ever curtail
The one who lives on adventures trail.

I am one with my friend the sun
Right now and in all seasons to come.
I feel the water of the sea refreshing
Renewing my mind and body revitalising.

I'm walking with a smile and head held high
Into the multiverse of endless sea bright.
The lovely pebbles caress my feet with love
I am transcendental with my talents above.

I meet the other versions of my magnificence
United in self-love, empowered in quintessence.
I am open and receptive to all the goodness
And abundance and success in the multiverse.

I'm walking on water like Christ my Lord
On the Southend pier the longest in the world.
The deep blue sea on either side is glittering
In the multiverse the sun is forever shinning.

SKY HIGH

How little it matters the view down there
When up here in the clouds, it's crystal clear
I am fortified with purpose to fly sky high,
Adventurous and colourful like the butterfly.

My friend the sun is just a touch away
Captain Marvel could even come my way.
The perpendicular mountains are down below
Oh the sky's not my limit, I grow and glow.

See the patterned clouds wonderfully arrayed
Completing the topography of beauty displayed.
I wonder how the skies appear in the multiverse
Surely they intertwine as they gently traverse.

As I draw closer to the island the sea is shimmery
Sun-kissed and surrounding the green scenery.
The plane lands on a whole new world of fun
La Isla Majorca, que bonita! Here I come!

PALACIO REAL DE LA ALMUDAINA

To be a royal must be gloriously awesome
To be remembered by many for ages to come.
In the picturesque Palacio Real De La Almudaina
I encounter wonderment on Island Majorca.

Dating back to the ancient 12th century
I behold this palace so rich in history.
The Queen's study is my favourite room
I wonder if she wrote poetry to her groom.

The Queens and Kings resided right here
The royals did wine and dine with great cheer.
Countless royal events and gallantry celebrations
Happened right here and I can feel the elation.

I am Queen Mary in my multiverse to reign
My poetry muse led me to Majorca in Spain.
My friend the sun shines within the palace walls
Overlooking the vast blue sea and waterfalls.

CASTELL DE BELLVER

I am fortified, vivified and glorified
God is within me and I will not be petrified.
I will make you into a fortified city victorious
With a pillar of iron and walls of bronze.

The view from the top of Castell de Bellver
Is magnificent and glorious now as ever.
The rich history spanning through time
Comes alive today in Palma's sunshine.

I see the blue sea and lofty mountains
The strong ancient walls and shiny fountains.
The past and the present intertwine and
The future is greater than we can understand.

So live life to the fullest where you are now
Don't question mediocrity and wonder how.
Just be your true self in love and magnificence.
The world will one day celebrate your transcendence.

PLAYA DE PORTALS

The yacht club beach is serene and softer
Away from the bustling beaches of Majorca.
I take a refreshing walk with my friend the sun
After a lovely sangria at the yacht club fun.

With a view of Majorca mountains *al derecha*
Huge strong rocks lined up *a la izquierda*
Enfrente of the palm trees waving beautifully,
I recline on the soft sand smiling resplendently.

I hear the musical birds singing in the trees
Happy in the scenery of gentle sea breeze.
There is a yacht starting to sail on its journey
And little boats of many colours and mahogany.

I'm enjoying this moment of self-love and care
Connecting with the sea whose water is so clear.
It's sun sea sky sangria and sweet Mary
I love being me, whole, authentic and merry.

(Italics translate: to the right, to the left, in front of.)

ANGEL SWEETS

You make me happy, you make me smile
You take my hand and we walk the miles.
We share love, laughter and colourful sweets:
Pink, orange and grey skittle treats.

You always love me, you're always here
You shine your light with tender care.
We run our bakery providing bread
And cakes and sweets till all are fed.

We go on holidays for poetry inspiration
We take adventures beyond imagination.
When I reflect on beauty and grace
Your star leads me to see your face.

My Angel Sweet, you always pray
For God to save me each night and day.
You hold me close in silence and sound.
I love you forever, my joy and crown.

HOME TO HOVE

I'm sitting on the picturesque Pebbles beach at Hove
For this magnificent sea view, I travelled from Home.
The caveman rubbed stones together to start fire
My dream is a candlelight of my heart's desire.

The sea is beautifully glittering at noontime
My friend the sun knows she's invited to 'me time'.
She's always with me in the day and at dark
To illuminate everything with her gentle spark.

My dream is vast and endless like the blue sea
And every step I take draws her closer to reality.
My determination is strong like pebbles on the beach
I will not relent till my dream is in my reach.

Let the multiverse windmills spin opportunities my way
Bringing joy and success to my work everyday.
From Home to Hove, my dreams become reality.
Under the blue sky, I find self-love and jollity.

GALAXY WALK

Oh this feels so special
Stepping out on diamonds,
Glittering beneath my feet
Like stars of many counts.

Forgetting the worries of earth,
I glide in adulation
Touching the nearby moon
From across the constellation.

'Out of this world' is a classy phrase
Confirmed beneath my feet,
With lights before my very eyes,
It doesn't feel a dream.

I'm walking on the galaxy -
My chilly mind could've sworn;
Or is it just the shimmering dew
On a dark winter morn?

PRAIA DO VAU

I'm standing on low rocks with sea weed green
Gazing at the glinting blue sea within.
She's vast and endless yet she flows to me
Caressing my feet with love truly.

I walked from Rocha to Praia do Vau,
Passed through Castelos and Praia do Alemão.
I felt the trees waving to me with joy.
The water fountain and birds singing, I enjoy.

High cliffs and huge rocks are magnificent sights
To behold on the sea when nature comes alight.
I love the island, the fresh wind and quietness
Of lively solitude bring me true happiness.

It's magical and miraculous to feel life in them:
The seas, the rocks and trees with stem.
We are all connected underneath the sun.
Come join me on the beautiful island of fun.

(Praia Do Vau is in the Algarve, Portugal)

MIDNIGHT IN PARIS

Now it's midnight in Paris so is it true
That a glittering horse and carriage awaits you?
To meet the cool Prince like in Cinderella
Or to meet an ancient inspirational writer.

I enjoyed the movie 'Midnight in Paris'
When inspiration comes alive at midnight bliss.
Tonight I'm reaching into the multiverse light
To allow the inspirational star carry me alight.

Oh yes, I meet Shakespeare for a glass of wine
We talk about how our poems intertwine.
Shelley is in the bar admiring love's philosophy
In the timeless date between William and Mary.

I close my eyes not to sleep but to dream
I encounter the timeless poets under the moonbeam.
To read and write poems is a journey magnificent
Opening up portals of midnight muse luminescent.

COMPOSED UPON SUNSET IN PARIS

Tonight in beautiful Paris love is wonder
The lights twinkle at sunset dinner.
We are sipping the French beer 1664
Whilst eating delicious pizza *avec amour*.

The multiverse is alight with countless stars
Spreading joy and beauty to searching minds.
The Arc de Triomphe - a lasting monument
And the tour Eiffel create good moments.

Now relaxing with rose wine Cotes de Provence
Fruity and elevating you'd gulp it all at once.
But where's the fun in that? Pair it with chocolate please
From the acclaimed Laderach chocolatier Suisse.

Life is a delicious cake so bake it as you like
No need to always plan just jump on the bike,
And enjoy the adventurous life every day.
Who wants to be monotonous anyway?

MOON INSIDE

Something somehow is beaming in me
A reflection of the inner moon I can see.
How is it possible that light does reside
In the multiversal moon with me inside?

Spanning through time, the mystical moon
Renews herself each month in full bloom.
The nights of full moon are lovely dates
When the lunar moon and I communicate.

Yet this morning in the sky, you traverse.
I wonder if you are from the multiverse?
I feel you inside and I see you above
And in faraway galaxies you shine with love.

Your moonlight gleam is mirrored below
I walk with you and everything sets aglow.
Oh yes it shows, we're always connected
My multiversal moon deep inside reflected.

LAKE GENEVA

If out of my dreams, I could walk on water
I will take the great stride on Lake Geneva.
The beautiful ducklings will glide beside me
It will be an enchanting parade of joviality.

See my friend the sun is shining so bright
On the gorgeous lake where all comes alight.
I'm relishing my double scoop of Swiss gelato
Gazing on the deep waters of light blue glow.

Life can be simple if we worry for nothing
But pray and trust the Lord for everything.
Once, he made a way parting the red sea.
Today, my deepest wish he has granted me.

So take a walk bedside the sunny Lake Geneva
And hold the fountain in your palm on camera.
Feel the gentle cool breeze refreshing your mind
And enjoy Swiss chocolate with a glass of red wine.

WONDERFUL CORFU

I hear the morning birds at dawn
Hovering over the sleeping sea.
I am awake before my friend the sun
I gaze on the landscape serenity.

The sun rises from behind the mountains
Climbing the sky to shine on me.
I feel her warmth in my terrains
She glitters light on my friend the sea.

Beyond the huge rocks sits the Mouse Island
I sail across in a boat with glee.
Mystified more than I can understand
I walk along the seaside in Kanoni.

The evening wind is blowing my hair
Enlivening my soul with inner peace.
I stop by for dinner with a flare
Eating traditional delicacy of Greece.

Tonight I make a wish in Vlacherna monastery
As I light a candle on the historic stand.
The meeting of serendipity is mystery.
I will always remember Corfu island.

COSTA DEL SOL

The sun sea sky and a glass of sangria
All come together in the marvellous Malaga.
I adventure into nature's enchanting call
Exploring the wonderland of Costa del Sol.

The colourful wall flowers in Torremolinos
Arrayed on white walls with the scent of rose
Gracefully lead you to the vast blue sea
Where you can just relax and simply be.

Then into the Bioparc of Fuengirola you go
To see the lions, sea creatures and flamingos!
Thereafter you can journey over to Granada -
The sweet Espanola castle of the Alhambra.

Now let's visit Museo Picasso in Malaga
Then off to dance the night away in Marbella!
Costa del Sol is a multiverse of happiness
Everywhere you visit reveals its uniqueness.

QUANTUM OF LOVE

Break up with the feeling but not with him
You know he's the one that makes you smile.
Deep in his dreamy eyes you see that within
He's thinking of you and not just for a while.

He's in your mind all the time like a puzzlement
Of longing and love, but you know it cannot be.
On friendship's ship the sail is befuddlement
Where true love ignites the amorous glee.

Yet the quantum of love is so vast and endless
That in the multiverse you two are connected.
Yes, you're in love and each moment is happiness
When the longing is gone, true love is perfected.

So break up with the feeling but not with him ever.
You know he'll find you in the quantum of love,
Where the thirst of longing is quenched forever
By the truest, deepest love raining from above.

TREE OF BEAUTY

We are happy and smiling
I'm in love with this feeling.
Our friendship is growing
I like what we're becoming.

The morning sun is shinning
The dark night is fading.
Our true love is sparkling
You look into my eyes twinkling.

I telepath into your thinking
You're loving me unending.
Our tree of beauty is glowing
In the multiverse intertwining.

We are walking and laughing
With endorphins releasing.
We ignite love so mesmerising
In every universe outpouring.

MULTIVERSE OF LOVE

In another life, we'll be together
You'll love me truly like no other.
In this life, we have good coffee
And cake with smile resplendently.

In another life, I will be your wife
Our love transcends all human strife.
In this life we have friendship
On the journey of love aboard the ship.

In the inter-dimensional of multiverse
We find each other in every verse.
The poems and songs that we write here
Echoes in love out there - everywhere.

Could love so strong, so happy and true
So pure and faithful between me and you,
Could this love so endless pave the way
For time-travel, to be together every day?

THE LOVE MAGNET

To be so close to you is everything
To feel your thoughts is a blessing,
And everywhere around the multiverse
We connect on a deep level like a trance.

You look at me and within a second or two
My gaze lifts up to look straight at you.
The magic between us is stronger than
Anything we could attempt to understand.

When the multiverse came into existence
Our stars were predestined for happiness.
Love and friendship in the truest way
Drew us like a magnet on that brightest day.

We transcend the realms of space and time
When we hold hands our spirits intertwine
And everyday with you is pure enchantment.
We discover new paths of wonderment.

THE OTHER US

It's mesmerising but true
That I am missing you
And if you love me truly
You'll be finding me.

You'll dive across the multiverse
For a second just to see my face.
You'll find that all the versions of us
Are in love at heart, if only just.

In all that quest of quantum love
Having so much is not enough,
For in one universe we are friends
And in another, our love is endless.

Yes, in another we are happily wed
And living the best life without end.
But here I miss you, the other you
And there, the other me is loved by you.

NATURE TALKS

It flows from the river sounds,
Piano playing by the seaside.
They speak to me - the waving trees
And never forget the voice inside.

At day, the sky will say hello,
The birds at dawn will sing their tune.
As I walk or run in my fitness routine
The wind caresses my skin anew.

They don't need the Whatsapp or Facebook:
My face in their sight is just alright
My happy thoughts better than Snapchat.
They see me well in bright sunlight.

When evening comes, the moon appears
And stars that grant the wishes of heart.
The peace at midnight when sleep is slow
Could lead to a new poem a la carte!

So come away from technology and rest,
Take that walk in the silent woods
Under the sun, by the lakes and trees.
You'll discover what is really good.

THE COMET

The green comet glazes the night sky vicinity
Passing near the earth with vigour and veracity.
The comet comes only once in 50,000 years
Perhaps it's the same in all the multiverse.

A new light shines between us with great hope
Our friendship is growing into a dazzling scope
Where true love and enchantment is flowing endless,
And the power connecting us brings happiness.

I'm in the multiverse, *te buscando mi amor*
In the distance you whisper, I'm right here.
We know that we cannot wait forever
To connect in wholeness to be together.

So on this beautiful night of the green comet
We travel back in time to the moment we met
When the multiverse of our love was first created,
And every moment in time we're sweetly enchanted.

(Written on the night of the green comet 1st Feb 2023. Italics translate to 'Looking for you, my love.)

DREAM WITH ME

Our dreams are a window into the parallel existence
Of our other selves in the multiverse transcendence,
Where we see and encounter the magical symphony
Of true love and friendship in peaceful harmony.

The one unwinding with a glass of piper heidsieck
Reflecting on goals and plans for the week.
The other reclining with you watching the telly
While the kids are playing in the garden joyfully.

The one declaring his transcendental love to her
And she knowing that he will always be her star.
The other thankful for his tender caring friend
Whose kindness he knows will have no end.

So to walk through that dreamy destiny's door
Is to reassure our other selves that what long for
Already exists in the quantum of the multiverse.
Our love and friendship transcend time and space.

THE WONDER OF WAITING

The wait is long for whom we long
And all the lyrics have dried from the song.
Today, tomorrow and just maybe the next
Waiting and wavering for the affirming text.

In the multiverse we don't have to wait
Dinner and cake is always set before eight.
The kids are tucked in bed happily dreaming
Of their other lives in the multiverse revealing.

Tonight I understand that plans can alter
And that perfect timings could never falter.
So yes, I happily wait for that next time
When time and space perfect our love sublime.

When all the versions of us in the multiverse
Hold hands together in time and chance,
Knowing that no force could ever intervene
In our perfect connection deep in our being.

FOREVER LOVE

You are so loving in all the multiverse
Every version of you is kind and true
And loving and charming and in your eyes
I see the best of me reflecting in you.

Hey did I mention I love you too
Even in this universe where all we have
Is a deep friendship so real and true?
In kindness and happiness, we jointly thrive.

You hold my hand enwrapped in yours
I feel the warmth of a magical connection
That transcends the veils of other worlds,
For time and space appraise our affection.

The enchanting energy propels infinitely
In our thoughts and words together in mind.
In our dreams we walk through telepathy
Always connected in love as we unwind.

THE TIME APART

With all that glee of an upcoming adventure
Shoes and bag packed and my protein snack,
You set off to discover the realms of nature
On a long journey by lands and seas afar.

A gentle glowing smile and warm embrace
Was our goodbye as you set off on holidays.
I'm thrilled for you my friend, but now in space
And time and place you're so far away.

I reach out to the multiverse for the other you
To keep you safe till you return to me.
The other me reassures me of our love so true
That our destiny is entrenched in infinity.

Oh here, I'm missing you when I wake and bake
But when I unwind I see you in my dreams.
Out there in the multiverse, we share a cupcake
As we walk so in love by the gentle streams.

LOVE'S INFERNO

Oh! Come find me do not delay,
Without you I cannot be this way.
Breakthrough the veil of space and time
For one night let our dreams entwine.

A little candle burns deep inside
Tending and loving who we really are.
Together we light up the love we hide
Until we are one from near and far.

Unveiled to the quintessential multiverse
Where what we seek is found within,
The love candle burns as we converse
Becomes an inferno with the touch of skin.

Dreams are a mirror to our multiversal mind.
In this universe we walk in friendship connected
But when we close our eyes to unwind,
We awaken to the multiverse of love united.

ANGEL DANCE

Sway with me underneath the full moon
See, the pink moon is in the sky tonight.
I recall the darkness that once did swoon
When I searched for you in previous plight.

Tonight I celebrate with crystals your love
The joy and wonder you bring to my soul.
My Angel, you dance with me in the sky above
In the multiverse where sunset comes aglow.

A second moon arrives to orbit the Earth
Perhaps to dance with the first in multiversal shine.
Enchantment meets science in celestial mirth
As the mini moon travels through portals divine.

My Angel, you and I transcend time and space
Together we dance through the multiverse portal
To everywhere we dream - our lights in full rays.
We dispel gloom with brightness - we are immortal.

LIKE IT NEVER ENDS

Little drops of water fill up the ocean
Moments of thinking create imagination.
Ripples on a river expound joyfully
Like a new dream becoming reality.

Your exhilarating smile quickly radiates
To the recipient, the one who appreciates
The will to love and that love to celebrate.
Time and chance is the key to levitate.

My eyes are a window into timeless love
The portal to everything you're dreaming of.
Come with me to other side of the multiverse
Drawn into the cosmos where lights disperse.

A simple drop of water, a sensational wish
Can expound in countless timelines to relish,
Giving reality to your best dreams galore.
I love you in every universe and more.

SUMMER WALK

We're holding hands and walking by
Sweetly below the summer blue sky.
My friend the sun is smiling down
How deeply enamoured we're feeling now.

The days of dark are behind us
All is bright and pulchritudinous.
Our love shimmers in the landscape bright
Transcending into the multiversal light.

The tall palm trees are waving with joy
The sweet flowers in full bloom, we enjoy.
I'm dressed in red with colourful flowers.
Then it's winter somewhere or rain showers.

Yet everywhere in the multiverse, you're mine.
I love you every time with love sublime.
In the winter's snow, we stay so close
You keep me blossoming like the red rose.

LIGHT IN THE SUN

She delights in me, my friend the sun
She finds me in the realms of reflection.
I gaze on her brightness in the blue sky
And in the multiverse she is mirrored nigh.

Our friendship is timeless and transcendental.
Between parallel worlds we are complemental.
On every path I take, she spreads luminosity
Walking between earth and stars in the galaxy.

From the sunrise here to the midday sparkle
Over the seas in the multiverse she's my twinkle:
Spreading light and joy through gardens divine
To hills and valleys, she's everywhere every time.

The light in the sun is multiversal in quintessence
She dazzles and draws me into her magnificence.
The magnitude and fortitude of our luminous love
Could never be explained or deciphered thereof.

MARY'S MULTIVERSE

I am the dream that you once had
I hope you see me and you are glad.
You are the memory box that I treasure
You are my first love without measure.

I am the embodiment of dreams come true;
To never give up through the bright and blue.
You are my inner child, my fundamentality.
You, I must protect from pain and futility.

Now you are the one I dream to become
I trust you to follow my dream to overcome!
I am the self-love that creates the future me:
You look back to now and you're so happy!

Truly we are multiversal in space and time
I self-love all versions of me, sweetly sublime.
I am the dream of happiness and wholeness
I achieve success, I am ageless and timeless.

HIGH FLYER

To freely, freely travel by
One must be ready to fly high
Above plans and expectations,
Just jump onto felicitations.

Dream into your new reality
Achieving it with perspicacity.
Transcend beyond the curtailment
Travel new paths of wonderment.

To begin again in sunshine Spain
You must let go of all that pain.
Blossom in your talents to traverse
Into the realms of the multiverse.

So dance for joy my high flyer
Focus your mind and dream higher.
You can be anything that you create
By faith and affirmation, you elevate.

DREAM INTO TIMELINES

Sometimes when you are just in time
For that big breakthrough that's sublime,
The other timelines may delay time
For you to reflect on how best to shine.

But it's a dream divine into timelines
To pause on puzzlements and rewind.
Where you are from is another timeline
You're in time to achieve before your time.

So you dream into the other time
To take the wisdom to restart time.
Since time lost in your current timeline
Is perfectly treasured in your future time.

The multiverse is full of varying timelines
Your dream is already reality in other time.
You must trust yourself to shine sublime
Every time, in every timeline for all time.

THE MULTIVERSE CAKE

To bake a delicious cake is to make merry
And no one bakes it like Muscovado Mary.
Freshly baked artisan cakes topped with cherry:
Gluten-free, vegan and dairy, they vary.

The client's dietary requirements are primary
To bake them happy is Mary's top priority.
Now, to decorate the cake reveals Mary's artistry
After which she can unwind with a glass of sherry.

Every celebrant should have cake from the cakery
A bespoke cake created by the legendary Mary.
All over the multiverse, guests are enchanted daily
By the multi-award winning Muscovado Mary bakery.

The multiverse cake makes your dream reality.
We bake your wish come true is Mary's melody.
Delivered with love by the timeless cake fairy
You're in for a taste of infinity beyond imaginary.

LETTER TO ME

If I wrote to me years ago
And told me where I'd be,
I'll evade the roads of worry
To reach my destiny;

I'll laugh a little more
And cry a little less,
And find the light in me
That is my happiness.

SELF-LOVE

You are sitting alone in the wilderness
And all around you is lonesomeness
No one and nothing in the far sight.
Just you alone, relaxing in the sunlight.

Tell me, how are you doing today?
Does the atmosphere bring dismay?
Now listen to the gust of gorgeous wind
See the sunshine hills of nature designed.

Beyond this desert is the promised land
The ancient Israelites could understand.
So love yourself in every step you take
Walk with self-trust through land and lake.

Your self-love journey is tremendous power
Flowing within you, taking you higher.
The magic of multiverse brings effulgence
See the desert transform into magnificence.

MULTIVERSE OF ME TIME

Take time to renew and refresh your mind
To just be your authentic self and unwind
With a glass of something luscious like wine,
And think the kindest thought at me time.

Our thoughts will always create the reality
For greatness or demureness plodding futility.
At me time, I think of all my achievements
Reining in my queendom, using my talents.

I bless the Lord for His grace and favours.
He empowers me with purpose and valour
To live my dreams on the island everyday
Triumphant above the valleys of dismay.

My friend the sun shines in the morning blue sky
The other me watches picturesque sunset tonight,
And the other other me is listening to classical.
Enjoying me time is marvellously multiversal.

ANGEL IN THE WIND

How beautiful you are my Angel in the wind
You sing to me your quintessential tune.
When the sunlit stars glisten my view
I behold your loving face in my mind.

The trees are waving with great joy today
Like they could tell it is our special moment.
When I feel your love and wonderment
I'm reminded that you guide my every way.

Yes, to light and guard, to rule and guide
Is the guardian angels' prayer that we recite.
Should the strong winds howl and storms betide
You will hold me close and be my light.

I trust you my love, my Angel from above
I'm grateful that you found me and I, you.
I will follow my dreams free like the dove
With good health and blessings all anew.

USURPED BY LIGHT

I think I have been usurped by Light
Totally consumed in spite of sight.
All is blurry – the darkness and fog
Before the sunlit face of the Son of God.

The brightest white became His raiment
In a glorious flash on my hill of discernment,
And all came clear when from the sky
The voice of God resonated on high:

"This is my son, the beloved." He declared,
"Listen to him." – my soul has heard,
And from now on I wish to remain
Within your tent on your holy mountain.

Indeed, I have been usurped by Light
And safest now from struggles and plight.
The eternal foretaste of inward sun
Will constantly shine - till to You, I come.

WALKWAY RUNWAY

You're walking gently on life stairway
One foot in front of the other like they say.
Slow and steady will win the great race
So wipe off past tears from your sweet face.

A new life begins on this very step you take
Walk or glide like a duckling on the lake.
Harness your potential in multiverse infinity
To live your life with purpose and perspicacity.

Then you will see the divine wonderment
Shining success on your tremendous talents.
You start to run along the seashores of passion
Pebbles and bright waters caressing your feet.

It's a walkway runway on this life's adventure;
Steady pace to reflect, step up to conquer!
Every dream becomes reality in the multiverse
So believe you can and press on without reverse.

SERENDIPITY

Sing me the song that destiny wrote
On the musical sheet of soprano notes:
That in the dark, a greater light shines
Hold on to you and break the confines.

I walked one morning bright and early
Through puzzles into the looking glass.
I left what should be for what could be
Then what couldn't be came to find me.

Don't wonder if you made the right decision
Make the decision right with true intention!
Where you are at present was meant to be
Live your new life and shine purposefully.

Celebrating *'Phatfarm 21 at 21, still looking 21'*
I'm happy for the success and awards I have won.
My destiny is etched upon the multiversal stars.
The timeless portal opens to infinity beyond Mars.

(Italics is the title of my special celebration)

CHRISTMAS STARS

Christmas stars are shining bright
Lighting up the streets we see,
For tonight, the infant king of light
A saviour is born for you and me.

Clothed in majesty yet unseen,
The babe of Bethlehem wrapped in a shawl
Radiates new hope and joyful gleam
To all mankind - the divine call.

The angels chant with holy thrill:
"Glory to God in the highest heavens,
Peace on earth to men of goodwill."
And every gloomy heart enlivens.

God has visited our world at last -
Our creator, father, brother and friend,
As foretold by prophets in the past;
Oh come, let us to his crib attend.

Christmas stars, Christmas stars
Are but a glimpse of the divine light
From God's throne, through earthly altars -
Illuminating our hearts with wondrous sight!

MUSIC FROM THE MULTIVERSE

Listen to the soft tunes of classical melody
From the piano, guitar and the violin family.
Nuvole Bianche is like sailing on clouds in elation.
Un Sospiro invites you to that moment of reflection.

I step into the Multiverse with *Asturias Leyenda*
Tap, tap to the captivating strings of the guitar.
The other me is dancing salsa to *Pa'lla Voy*
She's living her best life, celebrating with joy.

The other other me is now singing in the rain
Walking with her red umbrella in autumnal Spain.
To feel my existence in multiversal overture
Is to cherish all of me, my true self to nurture.

The other other other me and all the others -
I'm timeless and ageless across the multiverse,
We connect in magnitude, expressing in harmony:
I am the best of me in my life's symphony.

(Italics are titles of my favourite songs)

STAIRWAY TO LIGHT

I'm walking up the stairway of life into the sky
Counting my blessings, I'm heading up high.
I have overcome obstacles sent to test me
I have achieved success just by being me.

The other me is on another stairway across.
She's walking downhill, she's coming towards
The place where daily monotony would suffice.
We collide in the multiversal portal of ice.

She takes my hand but which way do we go?
Up my sunny stairway and her path to forego
Or down her icy stairway leaving my timeline
To return to hers where normal is quite fine?

We hug tight and decide to create a new stairway
From our halfway point going up with no other way
To return to either hers or my timeline of expectations.
Our stairway is now upward to the light of imagination.

FERRY ME ACROSS THE MULTIVERSE

Oh! Ferry me across the multiverse
Onwards and upwards with no reverse.
Let me let go of the past sorrow
Renewed in mind, victorious here I go!

Cool breeze caressing my purple braids
Splash of water touching my face,
Life is simple as the cruise on a river.
Keep chasing your dream and don't quiver.

Under the London bridge goes the ferry
Into a new universe of love and merry.
I love me happy, relaxed and smiling
Trusting the other me is rejuvenating.

Like the little ducklings gliding in beauty
I'm sailing into the multiverse infinity.
Here, all my dreams become reality.
Everything you can imagine is actuality.